The
Most
Wanted
Marketing
Strategy

for Exhibitors

The Most Wanted Marketing Strategy for Exhibitors

Steve Miller

Copyright ©2003

Printed in the United States of America

Library of Congress Catalog number: 2003112740

ISBN: 0-9655412-5-8

The Most Wanted Marketing Strategy for Exhibitors™ is a trademark of THE ADVENTURE LLC and Steve Miller, denoting a series of products and services, including consulting, speaking, training, facilitating, audio and video-based educational systems, books, newsletters, electronic media, web-based media, and other informational products.

Published by:

HiKelly Productions, Inc.
a subsidiary of
The Adventure LLC
32706 - 39th Ave. SW 98023
Federal Way, WA 98023

Order Information
To order more copies of this book, to get quantity discount information, or to get more information about Steve Miller's other products and services, contact:

The Adventure LLC
T 253-874-9665
F 253-874-9666
E info@theadventure.com
W www.theadventure.com

Other Books
by
Steve Miller

How to Get the Most Out of Trade Shows
(hardcover & softcover, 3rd Edition)
published by McGraw-Hill Trade

++++++++++++++++++++

**Over 88 Tips & Ideas to
Supercharge Your Exhibit Sales**

**Over 66 Tips & Tricks to
Supercharge Your Trade Show Promotions**

**How to Design a Wow! Trade Show Booth
Without Spending a Fortune**

published by HiKelly Productions, Inc.
253-874-9665
(all available at www.theadventure.com/products.html)

Hi, Kelly!

No exhibitors were harmed in the production of this book.

Who is this Steve Miller Guy?

Steve Miller is first and foremost Kelly's Dad, and Kay's first husband.

He is a student, teacher, and designated thinker of curious, forward thinking, and continually restless (defined as dissatisfied-with-status-quo) organizations. He operates a virtual strategic laboratory developing practical tools for applying the concepts flowing from his research and experience. (OK, he's a consultant.)

The essence of Steve's work is to develop creative and implementable ideas that create value propositions for associations and corporations. He has been variously called a change agent, alchemist, visionary, gadfly, and pain-in-the-butt. Some people actually don't like him, and even say bad things about him.

His clients are unquestionably elite, and in his own words, *"very way cool people,"* including many of *Tradeshow Week*'s Top 200 expositions and *Fortune 100* corporations:

CONEXPO-CON/AGG	Coca-Cola
Intl Manufacturing Technology Show	Boeing Commercial Airplane
PACK EXPO	Dana Corporation
Food Marketing Institute	Volvo
International Housewares Assn	Philips Electronics
Society of Manufacturing Engineers	Starbucks
National Assn of Home Builders	Precor
National Assn of Broadcasters	Cincinnati Milacron

...to name a few.

Steve has presented over 1000 speeches, workshops, and seminars around the world. Besides his five books, he has written for and has been featured in over 250 publications, including *Fast Company*, *Business Week*, *Fortune*, the *Wall Street Journal*, the *Washington Post*, *Sales & Marketing Management*, ASAE's *Association Management*, PCMA's *Convene*, TSEA's *ideas*, and *Highlights*. (OK, he made that last one up.)

You want operational efficiency? Call someone else. There are plenty of those consultants around. You want to move from insight to innovation to implementation? Call Steve.

The Adventure LLC
32706 39th Ave. SW
Federal Way, WA 98023
T 253-874-9665
F 253-874-9666
E mostwanted@theadventure.com
W www.theadventure.com

Table of Contents

The Most Wanted System

A re you a good exhibitor? If you answered yes, how do you know? There is really only one way and that is you have a *proven*, *measurable* method for connecting your trade show participation to your organization's overall sales and marketing objectives.

I didn't say you could build a beautiful booth or the biggest. I didn't say you had 23 years of experience and know how to handle every union in every major city. I didn't say you had locations right next to the front door of the hall. I didn't say you had the greatest giveaways or the biggest and best parties. I didn't say you were able to generate huge traffic - cramming anybody who could fog a mirror shoulder-to-shoulder in your booth.

I didn't say any of those things because the simple fact is they are *incidental* to the overall purpose of being at a trade show. And that purpose is to generate a high value in return for the investment you make. Period.

I remember my first sales job. I pulled double-duty as a student at the University of Arizona and working as the midday disk jockey on KIKX radio. KIKX was a Top 40 station, but didn't have a big audience.

One afternoon, the station manager called a meeting of all the DJ's. "I've decided you all need to help sell advertising time for the station. In order to keep your job, you will be required to meet a quota of sales for your own time slot. We'll pair you up with the station's salespeople who will help you."

Up to that point, the only thing I ever sold was the typical fund-raising stuff for my Little League baseball team back when I was about 12 years old. Even then, I wouldn't call it "selling," since my Dad pretty much took whatever we were pitching that year to the office and "encouraged" his employees to buy.

My assigned salesperson was a plaid-jacket-wearing guy named Bill. He'd been in radio sales for a long time. I think he used to work for Marconi. Anyway, Bill's big advice was to hand me a book - the Yellow Pages. "Dialing for dollars is the name of the game," he growled. "Start at 'A,' call everybody and ask if they want to buy some advertising time."

I learned much later this was the typical prospecting approach taught to new salespeople by all the radio stations. It was also taught by the TV stations, billboard manufacturers, newspapers, stockbrokers, siding manufacturers, charities, and now, apparently, every long distance carrier in the world. I feel really sorry for those companies and people whose names start with "A."

Of course, I lost that first sales job. Like the millions of new salespeople before and after me, I HATED dialing for dollars ... almost as much as the people who were on the receiving end of these calls.

The sad fact is that too many companies today rely on the good-old-fashioned "Dialing for Dollars" method for their sales and marketing efforts. This is especially true when it comes to exhibiting at events. Corporations blast preshow promotions to the entire pre-registration list inviting *everybody* to their booth. They design their exhibits to attract as many of the people walking the aisles as possible. They get stuck on the question,

"What's the total attendance of the show this year?" Like it matters.

It **doesn't** matter. Worrying about total attendance and attracting EVERYBODY into their booth is just another form of mass marketing. Or, another way of putting it – *Dialing for Dollars.*

After leaving college (and KIKX radio), I had a short stint as a professional golfer with the PGA. While I didn't have any more success playing golf for money than I did selling radio time, I was exposed to a new type of person – world-class athletes. And after spending a lot time with these people, I learned that much of the success of these elite competitors could be translated into the business world - especially the world of sales and marketing.

World-class athletes look at competition differently. They have a perspective and an attitude that is 180 degrees away from the average competitor. World-class business people and world-class exhibitors are the same. That's why they achieve world-class results.

This book is written to show you how to think, plan, and achieve world-class results at any trade show you participate in, no matter how small or large your organization or your exhibit.

This is not a How-To-Exhibit book in the traditional sense. Every other exhibit marketing book in print, including my own, has focused on the basics of exhibiting success – promotions, booth design, boothmanship, advertising specialties, working with unions, follow-up, etc. To be sure, some (including my own) have included discussions about setting objectives. But none have focused entirely on how to create a true, successful marketing strategy.

That's what *Most Wanted Marketing Strategy for Exhibitors* is all about. I'll provide you with a totally new perspective on how you really need to plan and prepare for your next event. The ultimate system is broken down into three segments:

What is your Most Wanted Objective?

Believe it or not, the vast majority of exhibitors at any show do not have clearly defined objectives. Oh sure, they'll say they have objectives, typically to make sales onsite or generate leads. But when asked, *"Exactly* how many sales do you expect? *Exactly* how many leads do you want?" they don't have an answer.

We set clear, measurable objectives for our companies at the beginning of each fiscal year, right? Why? Because it gives a benchmark to shoot for, a target we can plan all our other business activities around. It helps us create budgets, plan production, develop marketing materials ... everything. We say we're going to have $10 million in sales. At the end of the year, if we have $12 million – "We're going to Disney World!" If we have $9 million – "What went wrong?"

The same holds true for exhibiting. Without clear, specific, and measurable objectives written down in advance you will NEVER know whether you had a good show or not. Yet most companies don't know HOW to set these objectives. (And here's a dirty little secret about the trade show industry: neither do most show organizers. With the exception of MY clients, of course!)

In this section, I'll teach you how to determine objectives for an event that have true, measurable impact on your organization's overall success!

Who is your Most Wanted Target?

Imagine you are a manufacturer of "crumbers." (Crumbers are those thin utensils waiters use to scrape off your table between courses.)

Now imagine you plan to exhibit at the National Restaurant Show in Chicago. This show has 70,000 attendees!

Who do you sell to? Do you sell to fast food restaurants? Nope. Do you sell to buffet restaurants? Nope. Do you sell to the waitpeople, cooks, hosts, and hostesses who are part of the 70,000? Nope. You want the owners or managers.

What does a restaurant need to have in order to qualify as a prospect? They need tablecloths!

So, if you were looking for owners and managers of restaurants with tablecloths, why would you do anything to attract anybody else in your booth? Why would you send a big, bulk-mailing to the entire preregistration list? Why would you create an attraction in your exhibit that pulls in everybody walking the aisle?

The answer is, you wouldn't.

So why on earth would you do anything that attracts EVERYBODY to your booth? You shouldn't.

In this section, I'll share with you how to determine the exact right attendees to attract and why they would crawl through broken glass to get to your booth.

What is your Most Wanted Response?

Have you ever watched Joan Rivers on the QVC shopping channel? No? Well, I'll bet you can still answer the following question: what does Joan Rivers want you to do if you're watching her? Is there any doubt in your mind that she is totally, 100% focused on getting you to BUY her jewelry? Nope. Joan Rivers is extremely clear about exactly what RESPONSE she wants you to make.

I know for a fact that most exhibitors don't know what their *Most Wanted Objective* is. I also know for a fact that most exhibitors don't focus on their *Most Wanted Target.* I would also say that almost all exhibitors don't create a focused exhibiting plan designed to get their *Most Wanted Response.*

In this section, I'll show you how to make the link between your exhibiting efforts and your post-show short-term and long-term results.

The **Most Wanted System** is long overdue in the trade show world. Trade shows are still one of the most powerful marketing tools available to corporations today. But expecting exhibitors to continue to spend enormous amounts of time and money without receiving a commensurate return is a fantasy. You, the exhibitor, now have the ability to take control of your own destiny. You no longer have to depend on show management to deliver nebulous and unimportant reasons for participating at trade shows. Through the **Most Wanted System**, you can achieve the results and the value that you deserve!

The ROI Dilemma

Or *How to Stop Following the Herd and Really Get Value from Exhibiting*

What is it about trade shows and exhibitors? Why don't they see there *really* is high value to be gained from exhibitions?

For many years it appeared Corporate America was held captive by the annual "big trade show" in pretty much every industry you can name. Once a year, sometimes twice, every supplier and buyer was required to exhibit in or attend these events just because they had to be there.

And let's be real about this "required participation." It wasn't cheap. Not in the least. Exhibitors knew they were hostages to the multiple service providers in whatever city that year's convention was visiting. In order to get your exhibit delivered and installed, a hapless trade show manager would find himself or herself writing checks for any or all of the following services – exhibit installation and dismantling, carpenters, electricians, riggers, florists, carpet cleaners, furniture suppliers, sign painters, space rental, trade dailies, lead retrieval services, photographers, printers, security, hotels, shipping companies, and drayage. Attendees were marginally better off, but still had to contend with expensive hotels (who often conveniently raised rates during major conventions), airlines, restaurants, and any of the other miscellaneous costs related to travel.

Added to the cost of exhibiting and attending -- the dreaded

"Hassle Factor" of meetings and conventions. Long days. Long lines. Putting up with mediocre and indifferent customer service. Loud parties in the wee hours of the morning in the room next to yours. What am I leaving out?

"Held hostage" is the right terminology for what exhibitors faced. Nightmarish stories abound in this industry regarding the treatment they received from service providers on all spectrums. Is there a battle-worn industry veteran who can't share stories of handing out $20 and $50 "tips" to union workers during set-up or teardown? Maybe that's changed a little in recent years, but exhibitors are still required in many cities to hire expensive union labor for a couple of hours to set up a booth that's designed to be assembled by a twelve-year-old in twenty minutes. And despite the downturn in the nation's economy, too many unions still live by the 1890's mantra of Samuel Gompers, when he described the goal of organized labor as "More!"

In the "good old days" of trade shows, exhibitors could justify all the expenses and hassles because they could easily see the value of participating. Many events were "order writing shows," where a company could easily write enough business to cover the costs of exhibiting. Most corporations also generated high numbers of qualified leads, which turned into profitable post-show sales.

As little as thirty, even twenty years ago, trade shows were the unquestioned 800-pound gorilla of sales and marketing tools, and for good reason:

- Twenty years ago expositions and conventions were the efficient marketplace. All markets seek efficiency from whatever tools are available. That's Marketing 101.

- Communications were difficult. We depended on the telephone and the post office to communicate with our market force. Long distance telephone calls were expensive (remember WATS lines?) and the post office was slow. International communications relied on the cumbersome Telex machine. But that's all we had, other than physically traveling and visiting people.

- In many cases industry distribution channels were very regional, not national. There were no national chains to speak of. As a result, expositions became the annual location for entire industries to get together. All the buyers were there and they could see everything under one roof. All the sellers were there and they could see all the buyers under one roof.

- Trade journals weren't nearly as numerous as they are today.

- Corporations geared new product introductions around expositions, knowing that if they didn't introduce the new product at the big exposition that it might be another show cycle before they could really efficiently introduce a new product. They also knew it would be difficult for competition to copy and introduce a competing product until the next business cycle. So in many cases they would get a six, sometimes twelve-month head start on the marketplace.

Everything has changed over the last 20-30 years. Now we have a myriad of traditional and new tools corporations can use to communicate with markets:

Cell phones	Autoresponders
Fax machines	DVD
Fedex	Direct mail
Voicemail	Telemarketing
Email (text, HTML, etc.)	Buzz
The Internet	Pop-ups
Blackberries	Pop-unders
PDA's	Banners
Teleconferencing	Search engines
Videoconferencing	Linking
CD-ROM	Public relations
Newsletters (print, audio, video, electronic, etc.)	Promotions

... and, of course, trade shows. (Oh yes, and Virtual Trade Shows.)

The point is that all those really important reasons for trade shows to exist twenty years ago simply aren't as important today. This also means that trade shows don't have the iron grip on exhibitors like they used to. Markets still seek efficiency, but corporations have many communication vehicles to choose from that help do the job. Things have changed:

• In a recent survey, the number one reason why people say they go to an exposition is to see what's new. In fact, that's always been the case. However, corporations don't wait for a show to introduce new products anymore. If it's convenient, they will. If it happens to fall into the right product introduction schedule, then they'll use the show to introduce it. If it doesn't, they won't wait for the next show to come around. They'll find another way to introduce it.

• Exhibitors aren't giving as many "show specials" as they used to, because many events have moved away from true order-writing/sales shows to marketing events. Attendees, faced with a mind-boggling array of choices, look at events as their opportunity to cull out and collect information they can study in the quiet of their office later on.

• Because regular communication with both customers and prospects is now commonplace, exhibitors don't have to be at a trade show anymore - especially major corporations who have the budgets and sales forces to make that regular contact.

As a result, many of these larger corporations are casting a wary eye on the annual habit of exhibiting "large" in the big industry event. As mentioned before, trade shows are expensive, and those expenses seem to be exacerbated by layer upon layer of costs. Add to those hard costs the mentally and physically frustrating "Hassle Factor" of participating at a show, and it's easy to see why corporations demand an accounting for all that effort and expense.

There's a big problem, though. When you take an old, established event that for many years offered high onsite sales, and then morph it into a pure marketing tool, it becomes extremely difficult for corporations to prove measurable value.

Historically, the perception of sales is as a true measurable science, while marketing is more of an art form, and difficult to quantify. This creates the ROI Dilemma for both show sponsors and exhibitors. After all, it's imperative to justify the time, money, and effort invested!

So how have exhibitors and sponsors proved value in recent years? The most common method has been to simply look at total attendance as the new, magic bullet. For several years, exhibitors seemed to agree that was acceptable. After all, through most of the 80's and 90's, the economy chugged along pretty well, and attendance was high at most industry events. The aisles were crowded! And, as everyone knows, if the aisles are packed, then exhibitors MUST be having good results. Right? It tracked with the good, old fashioned advertising industry Conventional Wisdom that you can determine success by image and impressions.

Harsh reality struck when the dotcoms became dotgones and the economy slid south faster than Martha Stewart could say, "Sell!" The easy money dried up, millions of white-collar workers were laid off, and every organization on the planet cut budgets dramatically. Trade show attendance plummeted. The battle cry became, "Show me the value!" And trade shows became the new white elephant.

The industry "old guard" quickly learned a new skill – spinning. Press releases and promotional announcements touted the "quality of attendance." You could almost hear the gears grinding as show managers shifted from promoting total attendance to quality.

But despite all this backpedaling and spinning, really smart exhibiting companies have learned to see through the smoke screens and create extraordinarily successful results from carefully selected events.

You read it right, it IS possible to generate and measure success from exhibiting. The process, however, requires a total reversal of perception and planning. Perception is the start, you see, because it ultimately impacts the potential results you can achieve. Look at it this way:

Whatever your *Perception* is of an event dictates your *Attitude*, which determines the *Action Plan* you create, which then impacts the *Results* you receive.

For example, if your *Perception* of an event is that it's a very expensive waste of time with no results expected, you will then have an *Attitude* of, "Oh well, let's keep our costs down, go get this over with and get back to our real jobs." Your *Action Plan* is then driven by this, which ultimately gets what kind of *Results*? None! But guess what? By getting zero *Results*, you've reinforced your *Perception*, so it becomes a vicious circle.

Now, imagine your *Perception* this way. You believe an event has several thousand potential prospects and the opportunity to demonstrate immediate competitive superiority! What's your *Attitude*? It's very positive, which means you create an aggressive *Action Plan*, designed to maximize this great opportunity. A great *Action Plan* begets great *Results*!

Obviously, this is a simplification. The event must have a large enough quantity of the right target market for this to work. And you, the exhibitor, must also have the ability to connect the dots between the event and the ultimate objectives of your organization.

That's where the Most Wanted System comes into play.

In order to maximize the true value from trade shows and conventions you exhibit in or are considering, you must shift your thinking 180 degrees. You must understand the true purpose of marketing, in general, and then you must take a radical new view of trade shows (or, for that matter, any marketing tool you use).

Are You A Trade Show Flop?

As a consultant to the trade show industry, I feel like I've seen it all. Looking back to my first show as an exhibitor over 36 years ago, I don't think exhibitors have changed much. Despite all the new information available to help corporations be better exhibitors, they still look and act pretty much like they always did. And on top of it all, they still complain that trade shows don't provide any measurable return for their invested dollar.

This attitude continues to frustrate show managers. More and more trade and consumer expositions have attempted to educate their customers on all aspects of successful exhibiting, with mediocre success. Exhibitors seem to want to be able to complain about trade shows, but they just don't want to do anything about it.

Why do corporations adopt this attitude of apathy and indifference? I think there are seven reasons why most exhibitors fail to use trade shows as effectively as they can:

1. Trade shows are an extremely complicated form of marketing. In reality, trade show marketing encompasses almost every other sales and marketing tool available. Direct mail, telemarketing, trade advertising, the Internet, email, advertising specialties, billboards, TV, public relations, promotions, and literally a myriad of other marketing tools are all part of the trade show marketer's arsenal. A well-planned show considers all of them, and develops a strategy that utilizes the best mix. Most corporations never take the time to study the different synergies that may be applied, and as a result, never fully utilize the unique potential of trade shows. At the American Health Care Association's annual show, DRIpride Corporation combined eleven different marketing tools to achieve stunning success. Within six months after the show, they had generated a return of over 15 times their trade show investment.

2. Every show is different. Every show has its own unique personality affected by such factors as geography, total attendance, time of year, competition, state of the industry, total exhibitors, educational opportunities, etc. Yet most exhibitors approach every show, every year, the same exact way. For true success, corporations need to analyze a show's potential and then develop the best strategy.

3. Most corporations go for the wrong and/or unrealistic reasons. How many corporations base their decision to exhibit on total attendance? They hear that 10,000 buyers will be at the show and think they're going to get a few thousand leads. Yet, do they really have the plan in place or the ability to qualify and follow-up on that many? How many companies go to trade shows simply for image or because they feel their absence would speak louder than their presence? Trade shows are an extraordinary marketing tool when used correctly and realistically. Unfortunately, most corporations don't understand that the real measure of a trade show's potential is its overall purchasing power and how much of that they can reasonably expect to harvest. While several thousand attendees walked by, an exhibitor at WESTEC completely closed their booth for 50 invited visitors only. They went after quality, not quantity.

4. Most corporations don't know how to measure trade show success. When it gets down to quantifying the return on their invested trade show dollar, most corporations are in the dark. As a result, when belts get tightened, trade shows are the first marketing tool looked at for cutting back. Unless exhibitors know how to accurately forecast potential sales and are able to put a plan in place for achieving those sales, then the show doesn't get any marketing dollars. Throughout the short history of U.S. expositions, show after show has learned this lesson the hard way.

5. Most staffers don't know why they are there or what to do. It's common for exhibit staffers to receive little, if any, communication before a show. Too often it's limited to something like, "Here's your travel itinerary and booth schedule. See you there." Or sometimes the company will have a pre-show meeting, but it's usually for new product introduction and education. The fact is there are vast differences between working in the field and working a trade show, but most staffers have never been educated on how to understand those differences and how to work a show. The exhibit staffer is the most important, yet most neglected, factor in achieving trade show success. And the reason why is #6:

6. Exhibitors spend most of their time and money on the wrong side of the equation. I look at the trade show equation as having two sides: hardware and software. Under the hardware column are such important factors as space rental, exhibit design and construction, shipping, drayage, I&D, show services, etc. Under the software column are such tools as direct mail, telemarketing, booth staffers, drawings, giveaways, post-show follow-up, etc. Which side will provide a company with the highest return on investment? The software side, of course. Yet, which side do they typically spend the vast majority of their time, energy and money on? The hardware side, without a doubt. What's wrong with this picture? After U.S. Bank trained their exhibit staffers, over $3 million in new loans were written from one show!

7. Nobody taught them. Ask any exhibitor to think back to their very first trade show, and then ask a simple question: who taught them how to work that show? The overwhelming answer is — no one. So how did they learn? Odds are they learned by watching and copying other exhibitors. As a result, exhibitors tend to look and act alike. Competition at trade shows doesn't breed creativity and innovation. It breeds conformity.

Is it any wonder there is confusion and concern over trade shows, in general? When you combine a radically changing marketplace with a basic lack of knowledge and education about how to profitably utilize this complicated marketing tool, it's amazing trade shows are as vibrant as they are! And on top of all this, there is still one more piece to the puzzle that needs discussion – *what is marketing ... really?*

What is Marketing ... Really?

Or *Any Pitch is a Poor Pitch*

Here's a question that will spark a lively debate at almost any business function: **What is Marketing?**

In researching this book, I found a number of definitions. *Contemporary Marketing Wired* authors Louis E. Boone and David L. Kurtz gave this one:

> *"Marketing is the process of planning and executing the conception, pricing, promotion, and distribution of ideas, goods, services, organizations, and events to create and maintain relationships that will satisfy individual and organizational objectives."*

That is a traditional textbook style definition. Seems a little heavy to me. I personally like what Philip Kotler and Peter Drucker have to say about marketing.

Philip Kotler, noted author and consultant, explains marketing this way:

> *"Marketing is not the art of finding clever ways to dispose of what you make. It is the art of creating genuine customer value."*

And Peter Drucker, the godfather of business, has this comment:

> *"When managers speak of marketing, they usually mean the organized performance of all selling functions. The aim*

of marketing is to make selling superfluous. The aim of marketing is to know and understand the customer so well that the product or service fits him and sells itself."

What gets in our way regarding trade shows is the fact that, historically, trade shows have been selling environments. Corporations design and build big, beautiful displays, staff them with their sales force, assuming the sales force will know how to generate value.

Salespeople know how to generate value through SALES, which worked beautifully back when trade shows were primarily utilized as sales machines. The objectives were sales and all preshow planning was geared around creating the most sales possible.

But as we discussed in the second chapter (*The ROI Dilemma*), since most trade shows have morphed from actual selling environments to marketing environments, it stands to reason the planning process, the implementation, and even the staff need to be thought through from a marketing perspective.

But how do trade shows become marketing environments? In addition, do trade shows even have value as marketing tools – especially to larger corporations? After all, if a corporation has regular, ongoing communications with a high percentage of their target market, then where do expositions fit? Coca-Cola has something like a 98% market penetration. Why on earth do they need to be at an industry event?

This is where the discussion of marketing in general needs to come in. To be sure, there is a lot of confusion about what marketing actually is and even what its role should be on a day-to-day basis!

Let's first talk about what marketing is not. Marketing is not sales. As Drucker said, managers often speak of marketing as the organized performance of all selling functions. That is still selling. On the flip side, it's also not unusual for managers to speak of marketing as a function of "image," or "awareness." Marketing is neither of those. Spending money on image or building awareness is God's way of saying you have way too much money. Creating awareness for your products or brand is useless, unless somebody actually buys your stuff. Building image without persuasion is malpractice.

Kotler says marketing is the art of creating genuine customer value. Sergio Zyman, former CMO of Coca-Cola, has a great definition; "Marketing is all about selling more stuff to more people more often for more money." I wish I had thought of that one. But I will add this: in addition to understanding the definition of marketing, I also believe it's important to understand the purpose of marketing. I believe the purpose of marketing is "to be on the mind of the prospect when the prospect is ready to buy."

When you approach a trade show with the intent of generating sales, you are purely looking for those prospects that are ready to buy right now. If attendees are shifting their use of trade shows from order-writing vehicles to information-gathering vehicles, that doesn't diminish the value of the event. It simply shifts the desired destination to a later date. If this is true (and I think it certainly is for most trade shows today), then the need to be an extremely good exhibitor is magnified. You can't just stand around your booth, offer a show special, and expect the orders to roll in. You've got to be more proactive.

As I've already pointed out in the previous chapter, corporations are questioning the value of trade shows in today's new environment. But how do the attendees feel about trade shows? In a recent study of over 8,000 attendees at several major trade shows across different industries, I learned some interesting facts. Let's look at a few of the questions and top responses:

Please rate the following factors on a scale of 1-7 (7 being highest) in the importance when choosing to attend a meeting or exposition:						
	1	2	3	4	5	6	7
Type and variety of exhibitors	1%	1%	2%	6%	19%	42%	29%
Face-to-face opportunity with exhibitors	1%	1%	3%	9%	19%	39%	29%
See new products	1%	0%	1%	2%	8%	28%	60%
Expand resources/Find new product lines & vendors	1%	2%	3%	6%	16%	36%	37%
Expand knowledge of technology	1%	0%	1%	3%	10%	34%	51%

If we look at the top two boxes (6s & 7s), we see that "See new products," is easily the #1 reason why people attend trade shows. "Expand knowledge of technology," comes in second, but it could be argued that that's another way of seeing or learning what's new.

But look at what the third most important reason for attending is: to "expand resources, and find new product lines and vendors." What attendees are telling us is they use these events to check out potential new vendors, too! The trade show floor has actually become a more competitive arena. Attendees may already have good relationships with their suppliers, but they aren't assuming anything. Attendees are using trade shows to make sure they're working with the best suppliers, getting the best solutions, and getting the best deals. If a supplier chooses to not participate at an event or not participate aggressively, they are vulnerable to the competitor who does put their best foot forward.

Please rate the following influences for stopping at an exhibitor's booth:							
	1	2	3	4	5	6	7
Exhibitor has a product/ service I'm already interested in	1%	0%	0%	1%	6%	29%	63%
Exhibitor has a solution to my needs	1%	0%	1%	1%	6%	24%	66%
Past relationship with exhibitor	1%	1%	1%	5%	17%	41%	33%
Competitive comparison with other exhibitors	1%	1%	3%	9%	21%	39%	24%
Giveaways	18%	15%	14%	17%	15%	11%	7%
Size of booth	14%	18%	18%	23%	16%	6%	1%
Celebrity in the booth	44%	17%	15%	12%	5%	2%	1%

Attendees are looking for help. They are looking for solutions and answers to their needs. To be sure, you might have a hot giveaway, or a contest for trip to Hawaii, or Carmen Electra signing posters, or a big booth, and you might generate traffic. But the people you want to talk with are not drawn to you because of those. They are attracted to you because they clearly see you can help. These people want to talk with you, not fight a big crowd.

If your perception of exhibiting is geared around expensive flash and pizzazz, you're missing the point of being at a trade show. You are there to talk with the RIGHT people for the RIGHT business reasons. You are NOT there to talk to the wrong people for no good business reason.

Please rate the value of these media in gathering information for running your business							
	1	2	3	4	5	6	7
Advertising in trade magazines	3%	4%	8%	22%	28%	24%	9%
Personal sales calls from suppliers	7%	10%	14%	21%	18%	19%	10%
Articles in trade magazines	1%	2%	6%	14%	29%	35%	11%
Trade shows	1%	3%	5%	14%	24%	37%	15%
Peer networking/Word of mouth	1%	3%	4%	14%	25%	33%	17%
Internet/Email	5%	9%	12%	23%	24%	18%	8%

Another complaint I often hear from major exhibitors is, "Hey, we see our customers and prospects ALL the time. We don't need to be at a trade show." Yet 52% of attendees surveyed say they look to trade shows as their preferred medium for gathering important information.

The single most important thing to remember about any business is that results exist only on the outside. There should only be one focus, one starting point. To paraphrase a famous quote: It's the customer, stupid.

The customer is not interested in what makes our lives easier. The customer isn't interested in what the most efficient way for a supplier to communicate with him or her is. All the customer is interested in is his or her own values, wants, and reality. A supplier's job isn't to build a better path TO the customer. It's to build a better path FOR the customer.

I will repeat: the purpose of marketing is to be on the mind of the prospect when the prospect is ready to buy. Trade shows are outstanding tools for helping a prospect or customer gather information, compare products and suppliers, get answers, and analyze potential solutions.

Putting it simply, the purpose of business is to create and maintain long-term customer relationships. From the customer's perspective, trade shows help them decide who gets that relationship.

And THAT'S what marketing is all about.

The Most Wanted Objectives

Or *If you can't SEE the target, how do you expect to HIT the target?*

L et's talk golf.

What's the difference between a once-a-week golfer and someone on one of the professional tours?

OK, maybe there's a certain level of skill and talent that separates them, but the fact is there are thousands of amateur golfers who have skills and talents equal to many successful golf pros.

The main difference is what's going on between their ears – the mental side of the game. And a big part of that mental side is in how a professional golfer simply thinks about the game.

Take a look at Figure 1. This is a diagram of a par 4 hole on a golf course. If you don't play golf, that just means it's supposed to take you two shots to get onto the green and then two putts to get into the hole. The lower your score, the better. If you can get it in the hole in three shots, that's called a birdie, which is very good. If you go above par, that's not so good. I've labeled the different parts of the hole.

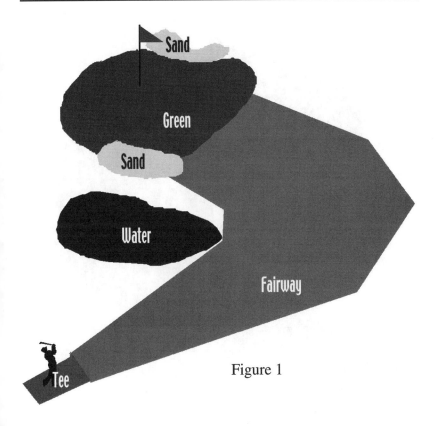

Figure 1

Now study Figure 2. Average weekend golfers, not on any of the men or women's professional tours, typically start out on the tee by taking the largest club from their bag, usually the Driver. They then take a mighty swing and smash the ball somewhere down the hole (#1). The golfer goes to his or her ball, automatically grabs a club and hits it off in the general direction of the green (#2). This process continues until the golfer finally gets on the Green, and then ultimately putts the ball into the hole (#3 - #8).

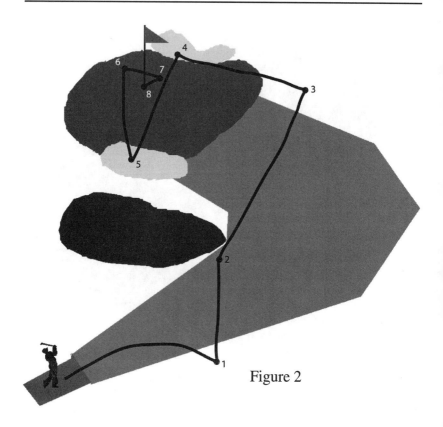

Figure 2

Weekend golfers play a game called "Tee-to-Green."

Much like these weekend warriors, the average exhibitor falls into the same type of trap.

It's a few weeks before a big trade show and the person in charge of exhibiting looks at her calendar:

"Uh oh, the big show is coming up fast! I know we've got the exhibit space, so where is our booth? Do we have a booth? What products should we display? Do we need to order tables and chairs? Who's going to staff the booth? Hmmmm, who's new? What about hotel rooms and travel? And do we have any old literature we don't need anymore that we can pass out and get rid of at the show?"

They finally get to the show, get the exhibit put up, and arrive on opening morning. Then the staffers all look at each other and ask, "So what are we supposed to be doing here?"

Successful, world-class exhibitors approach trade shows much the same way world-class, professional golfers play tournaments. If you've ever watched a tournament in person or on TV, you've seen some form of this little ritual:

The pro and his or her caddy stand on the Tee. Before the pro reaches for a club he turns to his caddy and asks, "Where's the pin?"

The caddy pulls out a small book. It contains maps of each hole on the golf course. The caddy turns to the pro and says, "It's in the northeast quadrant."

The pro then asks, "OK, so where do I want to be putting from in order to have my best shot at a birdie?"

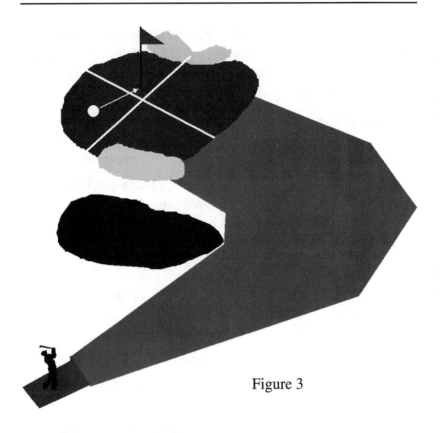

Figure 3

*They look at the map together (Figure 3) and the caddy
replies, "The grain on this green grows from east to west.
They mowed the green two different directions this morning
and then rolled it. The stimpmeter (believe it or not, this
is a real tool for measuring how fast a ball rolls) today is
reading 12.0, so it's very fast. I recommend you look to putt
against the grain so you'll have more control over the ball.
That means you want to be in the northwest quadrant."*

The pro then asks, "So what club in my bag can I hit eight times out of ten to that spot on the green, and where do I want to hit it from?"

The caddy says, "Today it's cold, so the ball won't fly as far as usual. There is a prevailing north-to-south wind, so under these conditions I would say you should hit your eight-iron (Figure 4). Under these conditions, you hit that club exactly 172 yards (line A). We also want to give you room for error, both front to back, as well as side to side, to avoid the sand traps (lines C). Therefore you want to be on this spot in the fairway (B)."

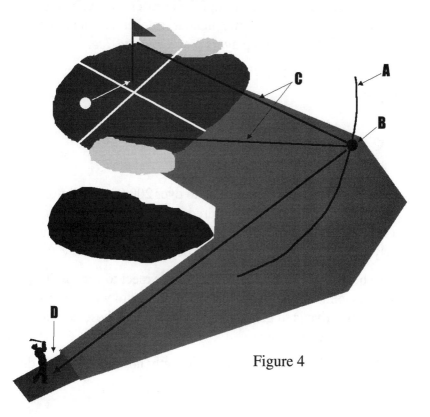

Figure 4

The caddy continues, "And from the tee you want to hit a three-wood, which will take you that exact spot in the fairway."

World-class professionals on the men's tour, the women's tour, the senior's tour, and the European tour all play a game that is reversed from the weekend, amateur golfer. They study the holes backwards before making any type of decision, or reaching for any club in their bag. They have fourteen clubs to use, and they can use them in any order they want. Nothing happens until they've gone through this process on every single hole and for every single shot. Amateur, weekend golfers play *Tee-to-Green*. World-class players play *Green-to-Tee*.

In order to be world-class, you have to start with this question:

Where's the pin?

In my experience, I've spoken to over 200,000 exhibitors. I've personally worked with hundreds more. I can safely say that less than 5% of all exhibitors at any trade shows will have clearly defined, written, measurable objectives for a show.

To be sure, if I ask people what they expect to accomplish, they'll respond with answers like, "We're here to write orders," or "Our objective is to generate new leads." And these certainly sound like good objectives.

But when I then ask, "Okay, so exactly how many orders do

you expect to write? Exactly how many leads do you expect to capture?" ... they look at me with blank faces.

Corporations start out every fiscal year with very clear objectives. Why is that? It's so they will have a target to shoot for; they will know how to plan, and how to allocate resources. If a corporation's objective is to do $10 million dollars in sales for the year and they do $12 million – hey, we're all going to Disneyland! If they do $9 million – what went wrong?

A corporation would never say, "Let's write as many orders as we can. At the end of the year, our gut will tell us if we did well or not." That's never going to happen.

The same principle applies to exhibiting. If you haven't developed clear, written, measurable objectives, you will NEVER know how well you did! You can't effectively plan. You can't effectively budget. And your staffers won't know why they are there.

In order to know how to measure results AFTER an event, you must first determine your clear objectives BEFORE the event. You must be able to answer this question:

Where's the pin?

You now understand the importance of clear and measurable objectives. Now you have to begin the process of defining them in a measurable way. Remember, it's not just important for you to have clear objectives. You also use those objectives to help develop your exhibit marketing plan. For example, the way you design and lay out your exhibit is different if you are primarily looking to write orders versus setting up hands-on demonstrations.

I became a student of exhibit marketing in 1978 after a major buyer opened my eyes to the true potential of trade shows. But it wasn't until 1988 that I developed the focus of generating measurable value from exhibiting. Ever since I understood the critical importance of objective setting, it's been the mainstay of my work. However, back in 1988 and through the mid 1990's, trade shows were HOT. Aisles were crowded. The economy was booming, primarily due to the Internet and all the Dotcoms coming to market. Corporations spent huge bucks on trade shows just because they could. And while I was certainly busy generating true ROI for my clients, I still felt like Noah must have before the rains came. Not everybody wanted to listen to my warnings.

But now that the economy has stalled, and especially now that we have so many other ways to communicate with our markets, trade shows are under the gun to prove value. Unfortunately, most of them have a difficult time doing that.

It's not that show management isn't trying to show how to prove value. It's that most people in the trade show industry are operationally focused. They simply don't know how to connect their events to corporate results from either a strategic or marketing perspective. As a result, when pressed, the advice you often hear from many industry "experts" or insiders is simply a spin of the same-old, same-old metrics we've been given for years. Here are a few common examples:

- Cost per impression

- Total traffic in the booth
- Percent of total attendees attracted
- Total attendance at the show
- Total number of brochures passed out
- Image and/or awareness
- Total number of people who can fog a mirror who managed to get in the aisles

OK, so I made the last one up. But let's be totally clear about objectives like these. They mean nothing; they prove nothing; and it would be extremely difficult to connect any of these to any meaningful results for your company. Any objective that smacks of nebulous hard value, like attendance, traffic, image, or awareness isn't worth the print on this page.

As we've already discussed, a trade show is purely and simply a marketing tool. And every marketing tool must stand on trial for its life as it relates to the goals and objectives of the corporation. Too often, corporations don't really connect trade shows to their company's objectives, so they aren't part of the overall marketing strategy. This is myopic. Connect the dots!

So how can you set clear, measurable, and meaningful objectives? The first place to start is with a simple formula I developed back in 1988. It looks like this:

A. Total hours of the show	
B. Average # of staffers on duty each hour	
C. Total staff/hours (A x B)	
D. Average # of quality conversations/hour	
E. Total # quality conversations (C x D)	

Pretty simple, but let's look at each one:

- Total hours of the show – How many hours is the show floor open during the entire event?
- Average # of staffers on duty each hour – How many staffers will be working your booth on average during each hour of the show?
- Total staff/hours – Multiply A times B.
- Average # of quality conversations per hour – How many quality conversations do you think each staffer will be able to have on average during each hour of the show? This might be a little tricky.

You'll notice I'm not asking how many encounters he or she will have. It's how many *quality* encounters. Talking with somebody who does not fit your target market is a waste of time, which I'll discuss more in the next chapter. What I need to define here, though, is the amount of time I think a staffer will need to spend with a qualified attendee.

Here's where a trade show myth can derail you. How many minutes do you think the average encounter is with an attendee? If you're like most of the 200,000 plus exhibitors I've spoken to, you're probably thinking it's somewhere between 3-5 minutes. However, in my national survey mentioned in the last chapter, those 8,000+ attendees told me the average quality encounter is 18.25 minutes! What's wrong with this picture?

Exhibitors tend to think about a show encounter from a "hit and run" perspective. Get 'em in and get 'em out. Attendees, on the other hand, are saying to exhibitors, "Give me a reason and I'll give you the time." If you've got a qualified and interested prospect who is willing to give you the time to show how your products or services will help them, then why would you want to end that conversation quickly? You wouldn't.

With this in mind, you will want to be very realistic about the potential number of quality conversations your staffers can average each hour. It might only be two or three, at most, if you take into consideration time spent with nonqualified attendees! You certainly may be able to generate more, but this is a good starting point for planning.

- Total # quality conversations – Multiply C times D.

Look at an example of how this might work:

A. Total hours of the show	20
B. Average # of staffers on duty each hour	4
C. Total staff/hours (A x B)	80
D. Average # of quality conversations/hour	3
E. Total # quality conversations (C x D)	240

Based on an event that is open for a total of 20 hours, with four staffers working the booth, that gives you a total of 80 staff/hours. Then if you project an average of three quality conversations per hour, you'll generate 240 quality conversations for the entire show. Of course, this is just an example. You very well might be able to generate more than three quality conversations per hour. And for some organizations in some industries, it might be less.

Is the glass half full or half empty?

240 quality conversations may sound low to a lot of exhibitors. "Hey, we've always generated a couple thousand prospects at this show every year! We'd never be satisfied with only 240!"

Yeah, well, let's look at reality. First off, those "couple

thousand prospects" you generated were more likely a couple thousand "suspects." In other words, you suspected they might be prospects. They were collected in the typical way – quick 3-minute conversations, fishbowl drawings, easy giveaways, or contests. Do any of these sound familiar?

What you have to do is look at exhibiting from a different perspective. How much are 240 quality leads worth to your company? What's your closing rate? If you can close 10% or 20% of those leads, how much would those 24 or 48 new customers be worth to your company? I'd bet a lot.

So what does this simple little formula tell us, and what can we do with it? We must recognize that there are basically two factors influencing our results. The first is the number of staffers working the booth. The second is the number of quality conversations they can have, which I already discussed.

The number of staffers is based on the available working space in your exhibit. Over the years, the industry has learned that an effective staffer needs a minimum of 40 net square feet of space. That allows room for a staffer and an attendee. In order to have four staffers working, you would need at least 160 net square feet of available working space for them. That does not include displays, products, tables, kiosks, etc., so those need to be included. Obviously, if you have room for more staffers, your potential results will go up. Using our example, doubling the number of staffers should double the results. That assumes, of course, your staffers know what they're doing!

Now let me ask you this: what commonly referred-to number is nowhere in the formula? Total attendance! Look at the formula and tell me how total attendance impacts the potential results. The fact is, it doesn't. The show might have 1000 attendees. It might have 10,000 attendees. It might have 100,000 attendees! None of those impact the formula.

So why the big focus on total attendance? It all falls back on the inability of exhibitors to measure their success and the frequent inability of show management to educate exhibitors about the real way to measure results.

Just recognizing the simple truth of this formula should start to change your focus from the typical exhibitor perspective of "tee-to-green," to the correct perspective of "green-to-tee."

By asking and answering the question, "Where's the pin?" you've made a huge step towards correctly measuring success at any trade show.

Connecting the Dots

Starting with this simple formula, you can extrapolate the numbers toward meaningful show objectives. Let's look at how we might go beyond the above example:

Write orders onsite

This one's simple. If we can uncover 240 qualified prospects, can we then close a percentage of them onsite? Let's add a step saying we'll close 10% of those conversations, which will give us 24 orders at the show. We can even go another step and say our average order will be $5000, giving us a total of $120,000 in show orders. Three clear objectives – 240 qualified prospects, 24 orders written, $120,000.

Generate post-show appointments

Let's say my sales force is capable of making 48 personal sales calls within three weeks after a show. My objective then would be to turn 20% of those 240 quality encounters into post-show appointments.

Generate permission for field reps to follow-up

Maybe the show staffers aren't going to be the ones doing the follow-up. You still want the attendee/prospect to give permission for a follow-up call. An objective might be that 30% of the 240 quality encounters give you permission to pass their contact information on to the field rep for follow-up.

A targeted percentage of the qualified encounters converted to sales

Instead of looking for onsite orders, it might make more sense to look at closing this new business after the show. Set a combination percentage and target date. For example, we might say we'd like to see 30% of the 240 qualified prospects write new business with us within six months. This could also be a tiered objective – 30% in six months, another 30% in twelve months.

Cost per sale

Take the amount invested in the show and divide it by the total number of sales made. You can use this whether you write orders onsite or set the objective for six months later. Either way can work.

I personally don't like the "Cost per Lead" objective you often see and hear. I think this is misdirection because too many exhibitors confuse prospects with suspects. If I capture 2000 names, my "cost per lead" might appear to be low. But if I only get 2 orders out of the bunch, then it doesn't do me any good. A much better number to look at is "cost per sale."

Demo a new product

Here's an easy one. If you have a new product to demo, you can set a goal of 240 demonstrations to qualified prospects, or some percentage of that group. I'd take it a step farther and set a percentage of those demonstrations that will turn into post-show appointments!

You can see that each one of these examples starts with the simple equation I showed you. There are certainly other ways of measuring success, but for the most part, they are versions of these.

What about current customers?

In each example we've discussed so far, we've focused on

objectives built around generating new customers.

The fact is that the vast majority of exhibitors look at trade shows as venues for generating new business. For some reason, this is another one of those historical habits we've gotten into.

But as I said earlier, the purpose of business is to create and maintain long-term customer relationships. You want to capture new customers, to be sure, but then you want to KEEP them. A trade show is an excellent place to do just that, for many reasons.

Look at it this way. YOU are looking for new business at a show, right? You might focus most, if not all, your efforts towards getting those new prospects. Oh sure, customers will stop by to visit. You might even pick up the phone and invite them to stop by. But for the most part, you won't have a master plan for them. It'll be more of a "Hey, nice to see you. How's business? How's the family? Thanks for stopping by!"

Now look at it from your competitors' perspective. Your current customers are what to them? They are PROSPECTS! And your competition is bending over backwards to create a good impression and take them away!

You can't let that happen. As part of your overall exhibit marketing plan, you must look at ways you can use the event to reinforce and enhance your current customers' decision to work with you. As a result, you need to look at how you can incorporate them into your overall objectives. I'll discuss this more in the next two chapters, because this is important.

You may want to take the formula and split the 240 projected conversations into two parts – prospects and current customers. If you have a low marketshare, you might look for 80% of those conversations to be with new prospects and 20% with current customers. If you've got high marketshare the ratio might be reversed. The main point is that you have clear, measurable objectives in advance.

Are there other objectives?

You can see I'm pretty rigid about making your objectives stand on trial for their lives. Trade shows are expensive! Even more so, trade shows take a LOT of time and energy. If we cannot connect the significant investment to an equally significant ROI, then they're most likely a waste of time. But once we have laser-beamed our focus and planning around these important criteria, we can look at some secondary objectives.

Conduct market research

Trade shows can be outstanding arenas for gathering market research. Maybe you're thinking about introducing a new product. Maybe you're looking at a new market. Maybe you want to learn more about the "pain points" of your customer base. These are all valuable exercises and may ultimately return significant benefits to your company.

But remember this: it's extremely difficult to connect these dots in the near-term. Conducting market research at an event may be a good idea as an add-on to the big objectives, but beware of making research itself the big objective. It's too difficult to link to any meaningful ROI.

Gain media exposure or publicity

Trade shows can be terrific vehicles for generating column inches in trade magazines. But once again, it's difficult to link this with ROI. If you received a good mention or even a positive article in a magazine that garnered 12,500 media impressions, well, so what? Those impressions may someday impact a decision to buy, but that can be very difficult to prove.

Enhance company image

Simple question: how would you ever know?

Create brand awareness

Let's make sure we're clear about this. Your brand is based solely on what your prospects and customers think it is, not what you tell them it is. Your brand cannot be transferred to their brains by a trade show exhibit. Certainly you can make promises to them regarding your products and company, but the customer will be the ultimate judge of whether you have lived up to those promises. That's how your brand develops and that happens over time.

(Both image and awareness are almost impossible to connect to any meaningful ROI. But let me offer this. If you do a really great job of setting meaningful objectives, and create and implement an effective plan for achieving those objectives, your company's image and brand will be enhanced.)

Support the association or industry

You're kidding me on this one, right? OK, OK, I completely understand you want to do this and I totally go along with that noble desire. BUT the hard, cold reality of business is this:

... when times get tough,

... when budgets get really tight,

... when people are being laid off,

... when bankruptcies are climbing,

... when entire industries are struggling to survive,

... well, your desire to support the association may be not be good enough.

As I said, all of these are fine as secondary or even tertiary objectives. The mistake too many exhibitors make is when they turn these into primary objectives. It's very, very difficult to prove any impactful value from these. It's even more difficult to connect the dots between these and any future sales.

My mantra in all this is simple: *Spend to Sell.* Whether that sale is generated on the trade show floor or two years later isn't important. What is important is that you have defined your Most Wanted Objectives that will ultimately connect to future business for your company. Once you have set your Most Wanted Objectives, you can then begin working your way back.

Remember the golf pro? The first question is always: *"Where's the pin?"* By defining your Most Wanted Objectives, you have a clear picture of where the pin is. Your strategy has begun to take form. But before you jump ahead and start designing your exhibit or promotions, there are still two more Most Wanteds left to be defined: your *Most Wanted Target* and *Most Wanted Response.*

The Most Wanted Attendee

Do you know who this is?

(Barney and Baby Bop are trademarks of Lyons Partnership, LP)

It's that cute purple dinosaur, Barney. Don't you just LOVE him?

Then again, maybe you aren't a big Barney fan. Maybe you don't love him. In fact, for several years I've noticed a lot of people who cringe and make faces when I mention his name. It seems that not many adults are middle of the road about Barney. They either love him or hate him. How do YOU feel?

But guess what? Whether you love him or hate him, ***BARNEY DOESN'T CARE!*** And the reason is very simple.

You aren't Barney's target market.

My daughter, Kelly, is eleven now. She's no longer into Barney. But, she's also no longer Barney's target market. When she was much younger, though, she was REALLY into Barney. You see, Barney's focus is on the two to five year old target market. When Kelly was between those ages, she was a Barney fanatic. She watched every episode of Barney -- thirty-seven times. She watched his videos. She had Barney on her bedspread. She even dressed up as Barney one year for Halloween. She LOVED Barney.

Barney is very clear about who his target market is and maintains a laser-beamed focus on that target. He talks their language. He becomes their friend. He sings songs they love. He teaches them. He bends over backwards to get his target to love him. And he makes zero effort to attract anybody outside that age group.

Does this focus work? Well, Barney's focus on the 2-5 year olds has been pegged in recent years to exceed the tidy little sum of $750 million. It works.

That same laser beam focus is critically important to your success at any trade show.

Just like Barney and my "crumber" example in the first chapter, you need to be very clear about whom you want to attract to your booth and whom you want to invest time with.

Unfortunately, because most exhibitors are caught in the Traffic Trap, they gear their efforts towards attracting as many people to their booth as possible, thinking this defines a successful show. But like Barney knows, it's the *focus* on the

Most Wanted that really makes a profitable difference. The Dodge Ram truck is a recent success story that drives this message home. Faced with a 7% market share of the truck market, Dodge hired an outside design company to help them grow. The proposed new design was a radical departure from any truck on the road at that time. Its huge front grill positively growled and scared off 80% of the participants in dozens of focus groups across the country. But Dodge was smart enough to realize that 20% was better than 7% and greenlighted the project. The 20% became their Most Wanted. The Dodge Ram is now one of the biggest selling trucks on the market.

Focus, focus, focus.

How do you determine whom to attract to your exhibit? If you're selling crumbers, it's pretty clear, but what if it's not that easy? There are criteria for deciding whom you should attract:

- *Is he/she in the decision-making loop?*

   You notice I didn't ask if he/she is the decision maker. In today's business world, it's common for more than one person to be involved in the decision-making process. It might include the person who signs the check. It might include the person who will be using the product. It might include somebody in between.

   The trap we fall into is thinking that everybody is somehow in the loop.

   Ask yourself this question: Would I make an appointment and get on an airplane to see this person? If the answer is NO, then you don't want to spend time with that person at a show. Unfortunately, many staffers confuse busyness with effectiveness. Just because you spent 30 minutes with someone who showed a lot of interest doesn't mean it was time well spent.

- *Does he/she have an **acknowledged** need?*

An old adage says to "find a need and fill it." I think that's bogus and I'll tell you why. I'm a strategic marketing consultant. I help organizations, LIKE YOURS, create innovative strategies that drive future success. I have dozens of success stories and delighted clients. I believe EVERY organization, LIKE YOURS, needs me.

Here's the catch, though. Not everybody agrees with that assessment. Heck, odds are YOU don't agree with it!

That means I have to first get you to agree you have the need. That's a hard sell. Just because YOU think someone has a need doesn't mean they agree with you. I'd rather uncover those people and organizations that have already made that distinction.

- *Does he/she have the ability to pay?*

I often find this to be fairly important.

- *Will a buying decision fall in your timeframe?*

As I pointed out earlier, if you're looking to write orders at an event, you're only looking for those people who are ready to buy RIGHT NOW. That's your timeframe.

You can adjust this to fit whatever you feel is reasonable. Maybe your product has a much longer sales cycle – say two years. Then that's the timeframe you work off. But again, the point is to be specific.

By drawing a clear picture of your target market, you can narrow down the segment of attendees to those who most impact your desired results. They're your Most Wanted. Then, everything you do to promote your participation is geared around just attracting that group.

Back in 1986, I was a guest on Robert Schuller's *Hour of Power*. Schuller is the pastor of the famous Crystal Cathedral in Garden Grove, California and televangelist to an international audience. I was invited to share my story of growing up with myasthenia gravis, a form of muscular dystrophy.

For two different Sunday morning services, I stood before almost 4,000 people in attendance while the cameras taped my story for broadcast to over twelve million people worldwide. Saying it was a big experience in my life would certainly be an understatement!

Afterwards, Dr. Schuller and I were sharing a quick lunch. He made the comment, "Steve, you should be a professional speaker!"

A professional speaker? Me? I didn't even know there *was* such a thing! "You mean you can actually get *paid to speak*?" I asked.

73

Dr. Schuller laughed and said, "Oh yes, you can get paid very well if you're good."

"But how do you find someone who will pay you to speak?"

He stopped laughing and gave me a serious look. "How do you hunt moose?" he asked. (I'll be perfectly honest. That wasn't exactly the type of answer I was expecting.)

I shrugged my shoulders and gave him a blank look.

"Well, would you go to Florida to hunt moose?"

"No," I said, "I guess I would go up north somewhere – to Canada or Alaska."

"And why would you do that?" he asked.

"Because that's where the moose are?" I responded.

"Yes!" he exclaimed. "Exactly right! In order to be a really good moose-hunter, you've got to go where the moose hang out. So, in other words, you need to understand as much about a moose as possible. They hang out with other moose up in Canada, so that's where you would go. You're looking for a LOT of moose, so you can increase your odds of getting one. Now what else do you need to think about when hunting moose? For example, would you hunt moose with a tennis racket?"

I thought for a minute and said, "No, of course not, I'd need some sort of big moose gun. I'd also have to use some type of moose bait to get them to come to me, right?"

"Absolutely," Dr. Schuller said. "The same principle for hunting moose is what you use to find people who hire speakers. Think about the circumstances for using a professional speaker. They could be hired to speak at conventions, meetings, banquets, sales conferences, trade shows, sales rallies, and many other functions."

Dr. Schuller's hunting moose metaphor works equally well when exhibiting at a trade show. Once you've defined your Most Wanted Attendees, the first question you would ask is: how many of those people will be at the show? The answer to that question has major implications on how you approach the event. For example, at the Society of Automotive Engineers annual show, Dana Corporation (a Fortune 500 company) defined their hot prospects as only *150* people out of the 35,000 total attendees. Emerson Electric (another Fortune 500 company) targeted only *50* people at a major air conditioning event. Both companies understood very clearly that they didn't need to see thousands of people to make a major impact on their companies. And by focusing on those extremely well-defined attendees, they were better able to plan for the events and create marketing campaigns designed just to attract those Most Wanted Attendees. They were hunting moose.

This brings up an important point about having a laser-beamed focus at trade shows. I often get the argument from staffers that if they narrow their focus they'll be missing some great future potential. "I could meet someone who isn't qualified, but someday they might be!" they'll cry.

In a perfect world, you'd talk with every single attendee at a trade show. You'd have plenty of time to interview each of them, capture their contact information, and then prioritize them in order of current and long-term potential. In an ideal situation, you may *possibly* uncover those people who someday might be potential prospects.

Unfortunately, trade shows aren't ideal situations. Your first big hurdle is TIME. Let's revisit our formula from the last chapter:

A. Total hours of the show	**20**
B. Average # of staffers on duty each hour	**4**
C. Total staff/hours (A x B)	**80**
D. Average # of quality conversations/hour	**3**
E. Total # quality conversations (C x D)	**240**

At this hypothetical event we have 20 hours of available show time. There's nothing we can do about that. It's fixed. So what can we control? We can control the number of staffers we have in the booth and to an extent, we can control the average number of conversations we have each hour.

What if we wanted to meet *every* attendee? Let's say there are 5,000 professional attendees at this event (this does not include exhibitor personnel, media, or guests).

Now let's say you can meet and talk with an attendee every five minutes (which is *very* aggressive). That would give you an average of 12 conversations per hour, per staffer. Still, in order to talk to all 5000 attendees for only five minutes each, you would need approximately 416 total staff hours.

A.	Total hours of the show	20
B.	Average # of staffers on duty each hour	21
C.	Total staff/hours (A x B)	416
D.	Average # of quality conversations/hour	12
E.	Total # quality conversations (C x D)	5000

By working the numbers backwards, in this example, you would need 21 total staffers working the booth every hour of the show! What if the show has 20,000 or 100,000 attendees? Obviously, this wouldn't be possible for most exhibiting companies.

The harsh reality is we must be extremely pragmatic about what we can accomplish at a trade show. It's impractical to think you can have quality conversations with thousands of people, so having a clear, realistic focus on who your Most Wanted Attendee is will dramatically impact how you plan for an event.

There is nothing wrong with focusing on a small number of attendees, as Dana Corporation and Emerson Electric showed. They recognized that the purpose of the trade show was to make a measurable impact on the overall objectives of their companies. They knew that, outside of the trade show, they wouldn't consciously try to contact all those people anyway, so why should they at the event?

Both companies asked the question, "Who would we want to see and begin quality conversations with out in the field?" That's who they targeted at the shows. That's why Dana only aimed at 150 specific attendees and Emerson Electric aimed at 50.

Of course, these are only examples. You must go through the same steps of clearly determining who your Most Wanted Attendee is, then be very pragmatic about what you WANT to accomplish and what you CAN accomplish. Before you decide on how big your booth will be, who will staff your booth, and what your booth will look like, you must first answer the question: who is your Most Wanted Attendee?

The Most Wanted Response

Do you ever watch the QVC shopping channel? Yeah, me neither.

But, just in case you don't know, QVC is a virtual shopping mall that almost never closes (only on Christmas). They began broadcasting on cable TV in November 1986 and now reach over 138 million homes worldwide. To date, 29 million people have shopped QVC, and they cover the gamut of products from electronics to jewelry to apparel to music and even furniture. Often celebrities will endorse products or even bring on their own designs. The George Foreman Grill was introduced on QVC.

My favorite example of a celebrity-driven product line is the Joan Rivers Classic Collection of jewelry. Joan's been on QVC for many years now, selling millions of dollars in jewelry to women who want to look just like her!

Whether or not you've ever watched Joan do her thing on QVC, let me ask you this:

When Joan Rivers is on QVC, promoting her line of jewelry, do you have ANY doubt in your mind what she wants you do?

Obviously, that's an easy question. She wants you to BUY

HER STUFF! Joan is very clear in her own mind exactly what type of response she wants from the millions of viewers. And because she is very clear about what response she wants from her viewing audience, she is very clear about how she talks to them.

This is what I call getting your *Most Wanted Response.*

When preparing for an event, it's critical to define what response or responses you want your Most Wanted Attendee to make both during his/her encounter with a staffer and after the show.

Think about the way staffers typically end an encounter:

"Well, thanks so much for stopping by. Why don't you give me your card/let me scan your badge and we'll follow-up with you after the show."

Sound familiar? Sure it does, because THAT'S WHAT EVERYONE DOES.

So what's wrong with that, you ask?

First off, our objective is to stand out from the crowd, not blend in with the crowd. If we do the same things everybody else is doing, say the same things, and act the same way, ... well, we've sent one more signal to them that we're all the same.

This is really important to understand. In the mind of the customer, everything walks the talk. If it looks like a duck, walks like a duck, and quacks like a duck, then it's a duck. Anything you do that quacks of competitive sameness, makes you a duck. And when a prospect or customer sees no difference between your company and your competitor, between your products and their products, then the buying decision boils down to one thing – price.

Secondly, when an attendee hears, "We'll follow-up after the show," their brains fog over. Put yourself in their shoes. They've spent many hours on a trade show floor, talking with dozens of friends, strangers, current suppliers, old suppliers, and potential new suppliers. They're on information and sensory overload! They may not even remember stopping in your booth, which is pretty common. It's especially common when they've had the same type of conversation with multiple exhibitors.

This has clear impact on the quality of follow-up after the show. I recently had a conversation with a major home construction industry supplier who said his field reps constantly complain about the poor quality leads they get from trade shows. Like many suppliers across different industries, this company has a select group of salespeople working the booth during the industry's big annual event. For the most part, these salespeople are asked to interact with attendees they will never see or talk with again. That salesperson is expected to talk with attendees, and collect "leads" for other salespeople to follow-up with later on. When the field rep contacts the "lead," they often hear the response, "I don't remember stopping by your booth," or "I don't remember asking for a follow-up call." Field reps begin to think all these "leads" are worthless.

As I've already stressed several times, you want to connect the dots between your company's investment and performance at a trade show with meaningful results after the show. You can set up that link through your Most Wanted Response.

The first part of your Most Wanted Response is to know, in advance, what you want your attendees to do at the show. It's not enough to want them to stop in your booth. Again, like your Most Wanted Objective and Most Wanted Attendee, you need to be specific. Here are some examples:

- You want a qualified attendee to share his/her top challenge that might relate to environmental concerns on his/her golf courses, and together with your staffer they see how your products might solve that challenge.

- You want a qualified attendee to try out one of your new hydraulic pumps.

- You want a qualified attendee to sit in on a live stage presentation of the latest technology in geophysical exploration services.

- You want a qualified attendee to do a blind taste test comparing your new fat-free potato chip with the top-selling chip.

- You want a qualified attendee to sit in on a virtual reality presentation of how your new drug will help kill cancer cells with fewer side effects to the patient.

- You want a qualified attendee to fill out a marketing research project for your proposed new running shoe.

Every one of these examples is geared toward what you want your Most Wanted Attendee to DO in your booth. That's the first part.

The second part of your Most Wanted Response is to

determine what the specific post-show action step would be:

- You want the qualified attendee to set up a specific date for a post-show appointment.

- You want the qualified attendee to set up a telephone appointment on a specific date.

- You want the qualified attendee to agree to attend your company's private event during the second week of September.

- You want the qualified attendee to agree he/she wants a full information package Fedexed to them within two weeks after the show.

- You want the qualified attendee to agree to a follow-up call from a field rep within two weeks after the show.

Why define your Most Wanted Response? The point is to be very clear about exactly what your Most Wanted Attendee will be doing in your booth and after the show. By focusing on these you create a "connect-the-dots" strategy that both you and the attendee agree to.

Of course, we recognize the fact that different qualified attendees will have different follow-up steps, so we must be flexible. But there is still a process that can be followed with each attendee.

There are seven steps in the Relationship Building Process:

- *Initial Greeting*

   Obviously, you need to have some type of human-to-human contact with the attendee.

- *Build Rapport & Qualify*

It's human nature to want to build some rapport first. People don't do business with companies. They do business with people! Some small rapport building is necessary to break the ice.

At the same time, you want to make sure you are talking with someone who fits the profile of your Most Wanted Attendee. During this step, your staffer should be asking questions that help determine whether this attendee fits the profile. If he/she doesn't, the staffer should quickly break off the conversation. Every minute spent with an unqualified attendee is money and opportunity lost!

- *Information Gathering*

If the attendee passes the qualifying test, the staffer segues into an information-gathering mode. The mistake most salespeople/staffers make here is to just launch into a TALKING mode. This is Asking-Questions-and-Listening time. What brought the attendee into your exhibit? What types of problems, needs, and challenges is he/she facing right now? What's expected in the near future?

The more information gathered at this time, the better positioned your company can be to help them. People also want to know that your company has their best interests at heart.

- *Needs Linkage & Demo*

  After uncovering as much information as possible to understand the prospect's situation, the staffer looks for some type of linkage between the prospect's situation and how your company can help solve it. This is where you would also demonstrate your product's capabilities.

- *Unique Solution*

  Your company then presents a solution designed to solve the prospect's situation. This solution should show how your company is uniquely qualified to help. In other words, you offer something that is difficult to get elsewhere.

- *Competitive Comparison*

  When presenting your Unique Solution, you need to also show how your company, people, products and/or services compare to the competition. After all, that prospect will go out and compare you anyway!

- *Mutual Agreement*

  If all these steps are carefully walked through, there is no "close," so to speak. You should have addressed all your prospect's questions and concerns to the point where you simply come to mutual agreement that you will work together.

Each one of these steps is critical to most relationship-building situations. You cannot skip any of them and you cannot breeze through one.

If you are a typical exhibitor, you think an average trade show encounter is less than five minutes. But if you've never met someone before and you must start at the first step, just how many steps can you get through in five minutes? You *might* be able to get through the Rapport/Qualifying step, and possibly the Information Gathering step. But this process takes time – a lot more than five minutes.

The objective of any encounter is to determine which step is the starting point and then methodically move through the next steps one at a time. With someone you've never met, you'd start at the beginning. With a prospect you've met before, you would start down the list, as you would obviously do with a customer.

But here are the two big points about a trade show encounter that most salespeople and staffers miss:

First, as long as you are methodically moving through the steps in the Relationship-Building Process, why would you ever cut off the conversation? This is why attendees see the average encounter lasting longer. If you give them a reason to stay and continue the conversation, they will give you the time.

The second point is this -- when you reach a step where you really can't effectively move on, then that's when the encounter should end. And this is important – at that point the "close" is getting mutual agreement to move on to the next step after the show. So, for example, if you determine that a visit to the prospect's factory is needed to gather the correct information, that's what the post-show follow-up step should be. Getting the prospect to agree to that very specific action is critical.

Think about how this process compares to the typical old-school selling method:

- Meet, schmooze, and small talk

- Pitch the product

- Trial close

- Overcome objection

- Trial close

- Overcome objection

- Trial close

- Body slam the prospect to the ground, and apply a Full Nelson until he /she cries Uncle!

OK, I made that last one up, but you get the point. Essentially, the two processes are diametrically opposed. One is product focused; the other is customer focused, which you can see by the time invested. Look at this diagram:

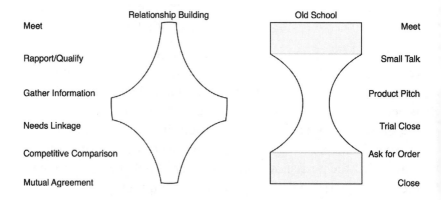

Relationship Building		Old School	
Meet			Meet
Rapport/Qualify			Small Talk
Gather Information			Product Pitch
Needs Linkage			Trial Close
Competitive Comparison			Ask for Order
Mutual Agreement			Close

The emphasis in the Relationship Building process is on Gathering Information and Needs Linkage. In other words, the focus is on the customer and his or her situation. Old School selling spends most of the time on small talk and asking for the order, not on the customer's needs.

There is one last thing to discuss regarding the importance of your Most Wanted Response – the establishment of TRUST. Here is one of my mantras:

People do business with people they know.

People do business with people they like.

But most importantly, people do business with people they TRUST.

Think about the longest relationships you have with your own suppliers and customers. In today's high-tech world, it's very difficult to create and produce a product or service that is impossible to duplicate in short order. For most of us, the intangible relationship with customers is the most important link we have. It's what truly separates us from our competition.

You may provide a great product. But I'd be willing to bet there are others who provide equally great, competitive products.

You may provide great service. But I'm sure there are others who do, too.

The reason people have a long-term relationship with you is because they TRUST you. They trust you will deliver the product or service you promised. They trust you will be fair on price. They trust you will stand behind your product. They trust you will tell them the truth. They trust you will be reachable when they have questions or problems. They trust you will take care of problems in a fair and expeditious manner.

The problem is that trust tends to take a long time to build. And in the beginning of a new relationship, how can you build trust early?

The answer lies in your Most Wanted Response.

By clearly establishing a mutually agreeable post-show follow-up step, you are, in essence, making a pact with your prospective customer. They are agreeing to continue the discussion on some level. But, more importantly, you are making a promise to them that you will follow-up on that pact.

It's absolutely amazing how many exhibitors don't follow-up in the way they promised after a show. At the Seattle Home Show several years ago, I was in the market for a hot tub. I personally stopped by eight hot tub distributors, and shared my objective of having a new hot tub in my back yard within 45 days. They all agreed to contact me after the show.

How many did I hear from? Zero. Zip. Nada. Not one of those salespeople I met with bothered to call me afterwards.

Unfortunately, this is much more common than you might think. I was facilitating a focus group for one of the top ten largest shows in the US, when the question of exhibitor follow-up was discussed.

"I always make sure to get the business card and brochure from the staffer I talk with, especially if it's a product I really need," said one focus group participant. "I do that because I'm already planning to do the follow-up myself. I learned a long time ago that I'm the one who has to be the adult in the relationship."

By clearly establishing your Most Wanted Response for your Most Wanted Attendee, you're setting yourself up to quickly separate yourself from most exhibitors. What better way to establish trust early than to make a promise and then come through on it, doing what you said you would do, and when you said you would do it?

As I've said, corporations today often have difficulty connecting the dots between a trade show and meaningful results. For many it's as simple as defining their Most Wanted Response. Like Joan Rivers on QVC, knowing exactly what you want your top customers and prospects to do both during their visit to your exhibit, as well as after the show, will go a long way towards connecting those dots.

What's Required to Make This Happen?

This may be blatantly cliché-ish, but the end of this book is just the beginning of the road to exhibiting excellence and profitability. Defining your *Most Wanteds* creates the bullseye on your target, or to use the metaphor of world-class golfers – the pin on the green. It's the high-altitude strategy.

Now you must translate that strategy into innovative, customer-driven tactics that will ultimately connect to the final dot – corporate profitability.

This is not an easy task. As I discussed previously, trade shows may be the most complicated marketing tool of all. Besides being a good strategist, you must also be a skilled advertiser, direct marketer, exhibit designer, meeting planner, travel agent, concierge, sales manager, web designer, trainer, customer service agent, creative director, and camp counselor.

But most important, to succeed, you must have a genuine, honest-to-goodness interest in profitability. Most people don't.

Most sales and marketing people think you just need to be louder and noisier. Most sales and marketing people think you have the make the sale RIGHT NOW in order to be successful. Most sales and marketing people retreat to "playground shouting" for attention instead of engaging in adult conversation.

Winning in business is a marathon, not a sprint. Remember the two important business definitions I discussed:

> The *purpose of business* is to create and maintain long-term, profitable customer relationships.

*The **purpose of marketing** is to be on the mind of the prospect when the prospect is ready to buy.*

While this book focuses on the trade show medium, it obviously pertains to every other marketing tool, and even business in general.

Why do people do business with you? Do you know? Or maybe a better question is: would *you* do business with *you*? Go back to the top three reasons why attendees decide to stop in a particular exhibit:

1. The exhibitor has a product or service I'm already interested in.

2. The exhibitor has a solution to my needs.

3. I have a past relationship with the exhibitor.

Have you given attendees a reason to visit you that is important to THEM? Have you given prospects a reason to do business with you that is important to THEM? Have you given current customers a reason to continue doing business with you that is important to THEM? Let your customers guide you.

Double-decker exhibits, gimmicks, contests, giveaways, stage shows, climbing walls, virtual reality goggles, celebrities, free food, putting greens, half-naked women, popcorn, and booth location may seem important. But they are NOT the be-all, end-all tools that make or break your show success. In case you didn't notice, I didn't talk about those much in this book. Succeeding at trade shows, just like succeeding in business, is hard! But to quote myself, "Hard is never a reason NOT to do something."

Fortunately for you, an incredibly high percentage of corporations view trade shows as expensive exercises in futility. While sitting comfortably in the back of their booths, they point their fingers at outside factors as the reason why never-met-before prospects don't push and shove their way in to write million-dollar orders. They don't consider for a moment pointing their fingers back at themselves. Bashing trade shows is so much easier.

Be different.

Be hard to overtake.

Be hard to copy.

What are YOUR *Most Wanteds*?